SUPERBASE 1
NELLIS

SUPERBASE 1

NELLIS

The Home of 'Red Flag'

George Hall

Published in 1988 by Osprey Publishing
Limited
27A Floral Street, London WC2E 9DP
Member company of the George Philip
Group

British Library Cataloguing in Publication
Data
Hall, George
    Nellis.—(Superbase; 1).
    1. United States. Air bases
    I. Title   II. Series
    358'.4'17'0973
ISBN 0–85045–844–7

Editor Dennis Baldry
Designed by David Tarbutt
Printed in Hong Kong

Front cover Is it possible to
imagine an airbase without the F-4
Phantom? This F-4E is normally
based at George AFB, California
where it serves with the 37th TFW

Title pages An F-16 Fighting Falcon
on long final to Nellis against the
warm colours of the mountains in
the background

Introduction

In the skillet-hot desert north of Las Vegas, Nevada, the US Air Force plays for keeps. Nellis Air Force Base is the most active Tactical Air Command base in the United States, sitting on the edge of a 3-million-acre aerial range where just about anything goes. Its long-time nickname is acknowledged throughout the Air Force: 'home of the fighter pilot.'

Nellis affords the modern jet pilot all the airspace he could want to turn, burn, and even go supersonic in an effort to get on his adversary's six o'clock. The desert weather (if you can withstand the heat) is another big plus—330 days of CAVU (clear air, visibility unlimited) flying every year. The big base was established as a World War 2 training field and was later named after a Las Vegas native, Lt Bill Nellis, who died in a dogfight over Germany in 1944.

No American base boasts a wider range of resident units and fascinating activities. The Fighter Weapons School, a scholarly Air Force version of the Navy's Top Gun, is headquartered here along with its own stable of F-5, F-15, F-16, F-111, A-10, and T-38 aircraft. Next door are the 64th and 65th Aggressor Squadrons, professional bad guys who are schooled in the emulation of the aerial tactics of potential enemies around the globe. Another hangar down are the Thunderbirds Air Demonstration Squadron, now flying red-white-and-blue F-16 Falcons in dazzling aerobatic displays around the country.

And there's more. A whole wing of F-16s almost gets lost in the shuffle at Nellis; at any other TAC base they would be the centrepiece. And four times a year Nellis plays host to Red Flag, a six-week mock air war between players from the Air Force, Navy, Marine Corps, and NATO forces. Every two years the mile-long ramp is swelled with 90 jets competing in Gunsmoke, an Air Force-wide gunnery and bombing competition. Other units on the base organize and administrate all this frenetic activity, including air wars and bombing runs over a desert range bigger than many European countries.

So slap on your No 12 sunscreen, and we'll take a tour of the flight line to see what's doing. A word to the wise: don't even think of visiting Nellis without extensive prior permission. It's a highly secure base, and even VIP visitors are escorted every step of the way by base public affairs personnel. Special thanks to our escorts and guides, who often went beyond the call of duty in Nevada's 110-degree weather: Maj Andy Andrijauskas, Sgt Chris Miller, Capt Barry Anderson, Red Flag's Col Doug 'Zip Gun' Melson, and Maj Mike 'Boa' Straight of the Fighter Weapons School. Let's do it. . .

George Hall has been photographing and writing about American military aircraft for twenty years. He's accumulated thousands of photo hours in over a hundred different military and civilian aircraft types—everything from blimps to the hottest Mach 2 fighters. His other books include: *CV: Carrier Aviation* (Presidio Press); *USAFE: A Primer of Modern Air Combat in Europe* (Presidio Press); *Red Flag: Air Combat for the Eighties* (Presidio Press); *Marine Air: First to Fight* (Presidio Press); *Top Gun: The Navy Fighter Weapons School* (Presidio Press); and *Total Force: Flying with America's Reserve And Guard* (Thomasson-Grant).

Photographs were taken exclusively with Nikon cameras and lenses ranging from 16 mm fisheyes to 500 mm telephotos. With few exceptions, the film of choice is Kodachrome 64 slide film.

Right The mighty Republic F-105 Thunderchief enjoyed a brief but spectacular career with the Thunderbirds Air Demonstration Squadron between 1964–65. One of their specially modified B models is preserved at Nellis AFB

Contents

The Thunderbirds

Left Immaculate Thunderbirds, immaculate parking. The team received their strikingly painted F-16s in 1982. **Below** The fine lines of the F-5E Tiger II stand out against the Thunderbirds' hangar

Home of the Thunderbirds

Below Thunderbirds' crewmen stand to attention as each F-16 heads for the runway. **Left** Polished to perfection, a four-ship of glinting Thunderbirds lifts off

This page Thunderbird No 4 slips
neatly into the slot position as the
formation climbs out. **Right** Smoke's
on as the Thunderbirds pass in
review, their station-keeping as
precise as you'll ever see

This page A snappy break for landing marks the end of a successful practice over the field. **Right** Thunderbird No 8 is a two-seat F-16B which is used for press and VIP flights. Anyone for 9G?

Air Guard A-7s

Gunsmoke 1987, the US Air Force's biennial weapons meet. These competitors are from the 120th TFS, 140th TFW, Colorado ANG. Each team brings four aircraft plus one spare

Above A custom painted baggage blivet on a
Colorado A-7D. The Guard unit shocked the active
Air Force by winning Gunsmoke's 'Top Gun' award
in 1981. **Far right** A member of the exclusive
Buckley ANGB *Mile High Militia* club; it's hard to
believe that the Colorado ANG'c spotless Corsairs
are nearly 20 years old. Interestingly, the Air Force
never officially adopted the Corsair II nickname for
the A-7D. A total of 459 D models were produced by
Vought

A-7Ds of the 112th TFS, 180th TFG, Ohio ANG, take on liquid oxygen at Gunsmoke 1987

The A-7D has 35 access panels, 90 per cent of which can be reached without an aircraft stand. US Air Force units gave up their A-7s to the Air Guard following the introduction of the Fairchild A-10A Thunderbolt II in the mid-1980s

Intruder

Red Flag players often include Navy and Marine Corps assets. Looking rather conspicuous against the desert, these A-6E Intruders are from attack squadron VA-95 'Green Lizards' in Washington State

Skyhawk

Marine Corps' A-4M Skyhawks of VMA-311 'Tom Cats' from MCAS El Toro, California repose on the Red Flag ramp. No matter what you call it (*Heinemann's Hot Rod*, *Scooter*, *Bantam Bomber* or *Tinker Toy Bomber*), the Skyhawk remains an effective attack aircraft. The Marines also employ the two-seat OA-4M for fast forward air control work. **Inset** Close-up of 25-lb practice bombs on a Marine A-4M

Warthogs

Main picture Lined up on the concrete, these gunslingers hail from the 354th TFW at Myrtle Beach, South Carolina. **Inset** From concrete to baked desert: an A-10 Warthog gets a tactical combat reload of its mighty 30 mm seven-barrel anti-tank cannon on the dry bed of Texas Lake in the Nellis Range. **Far inset** A new twist, seen at Gunsmoke 1987, is this interesting smoke deflector on the business end of the Avenger cannon

Warthogs as far as the eye can see (well, almost). Natty covers protect the A-10's two 9065 lb (4112 kg) thrust GE TF34-100 turbofans against foreign object damage (FOD)

The A-10 hits hard and can carry a total ordnance load of 16,000 lb (7257 kg), but this example is using only one of its eleven pylons to carry a captive Maverick air-to-surface missile for training purposes. In wartime, the aircraft would be festooned with bombs, Mavericks, jamming pods and even Sidewinder air-to-air missiles for self-defence

Above This A-10 came from the 343rd TFW, Alaskan Air Command to compete in Gunsmoke 1987.
Right Another 343rd TFW machine undergoes the trial of a tactical engine change

Below This 600 US Gal (2273 lit) drop tank was removed from a 25th TFS A-10 which arrived at Nellis from its home base at Suwon in South Korea

MB
354 TFW

AF
79 101

A-10 fin flashes: the identity of the machine at far left is self-evident, while the AK tail code tells us that this Warthog belongs to the 21st TFW at Eielson AFB. Note the Suwon-based A-10 in the background

A Nellis-based A-10 of the 57th FWW prepares for engine start on the Red Flag ramp. **Right** Much later, carrying an electronic countermeasures pod under the left wing, another 57th FWW A-10 slips into Nellis at sunset

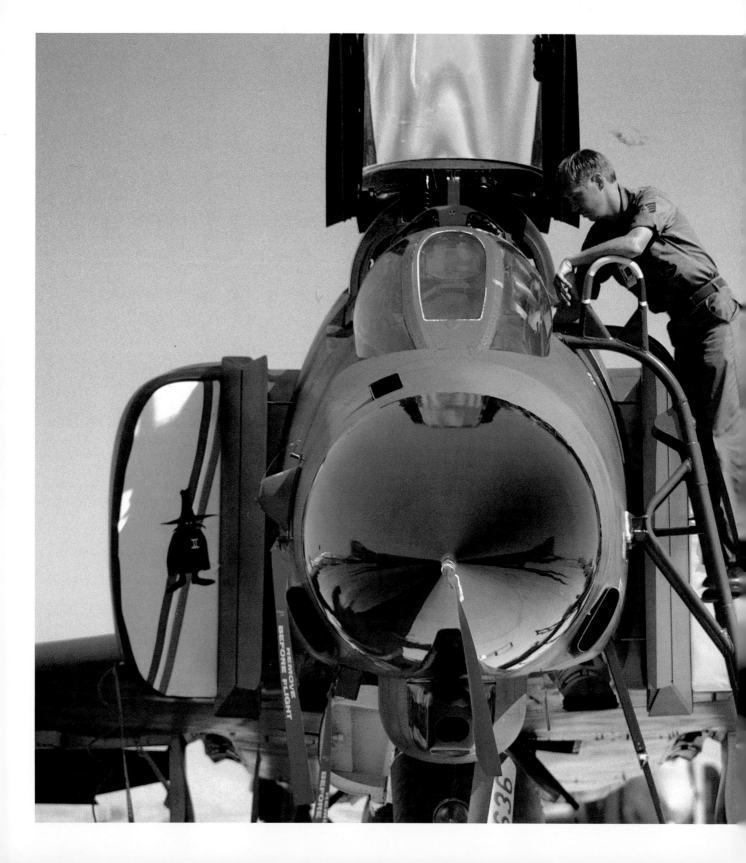

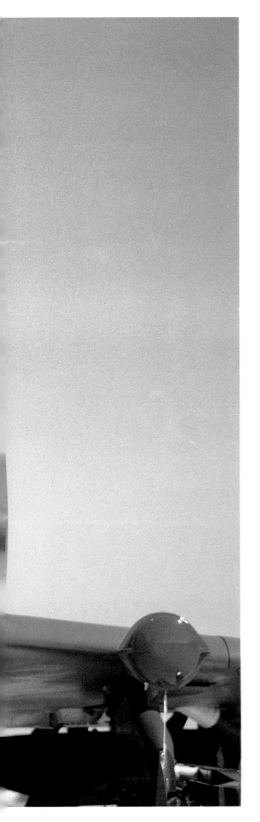

Phabulous Phantoms

Left F-4s didn't look this good when they rolled out of the factory 20 years ago! This absolutely pristine F-4E is from the 37th TFW at nearby George AFB, California. Note the 'Spook' on the intake cover

Top RF-4C reconnaissance Phantom visiting from the 67th TRW at Bergstrom AFB, Texas. The RF-4C is 4 ft 8 ins (144 cms) longer to accommodate the cameras, extra radar gear and other equipment.
Above Close-up of the ALQ-119 jamming pod carried on the left inboard pylon

Right The RF-4C is extremely sophisticated and demands careful maintenance. A technician adjusts the 'wiggly amps' in the APQ-99 terrain-avoidance/mapping radar

Main picture F-4E Phantoms of the 4th TFW, Seymour-Johnson AFB, North Carolina, stand ready for the next Gunsmoke event. **Far inset** This example has been busy with its 20 mm M61A1 Vulcan cannon

These pages A walk-around sequence devoted to an F-4E Phantom of the 37th TFW. The F-4E first flew in June 1967 and remained in production at St Louis until 1979

Canopy to canopy: the main picture reveals what Air Force Phantoms look like when they aren't competing in Gunsmoke! **Below** A crewman from the 37th TFW touches up the paintwork on the canopy rail of an F-4E

Typical hustle at Nellis: Gunsmoke
Phantoms taxi out, practising
Thunderbirds taxi in, and an F-16 of
the Fighter Weapons School blasts
off in full afterburner

This page The smart air defence grey camouflage is a world away from the original tactical warpaint once worn by this old warrior, an F-4D of the 924th TFG, Texas Air National Guard

Far right Weasel bird: slats, flaps and gear all down, an F-4G SAM-suppression aircraft comes in on final. The J79-17 engines fitted to the F-4G are not supposed to trail tell-tale smoke

These pages A clever variation on the 'Egypt One' air defence camouflage scheme enhances the classic lines of this immaculate F-4D Phantom, which is operated by the 160th TFS, Alabama Air National Guard from Donnelly Field. The AAA-4 infrared detector, originally housed in the pod under the radar, is no longer fitted to the F-4D and has been replaced by an electronic warfare package. In the light of Vietnam experience the F-4E introduced an M61 gun fitted in the nose, but other Phantoms (except the *Luftwaffe* F-4F and the F-4EJ built in Japan) have to rely on a podded version of the gun carried under the belly, as here. Polishing is clearly a way of life in the Guard, as illustrated by the gleaming tail of F-4D 66-575 (above)

More than 20 Phantoms are visible
in this Nellis ramp shot. Despite the
introduction of the F-14, F-15, F-16
and F/A-18, US forces still utilize
around 2000 F-4s in a variety of
roles. Thanks to Mitsubishi in Japan,
Phantom production reached 5201
before the line finally closed in
1981. In common with US operators,
many foreign air forces are
investing in series of upgrade
programmes to keep the McDonnell
fighter operational into the 21st
century

Phantom dawn: a Marine Corps' F-4S is readied for a Red Flag hop at first light. The Marines are not expected to trade in their last F-4s for F/A-18s until the 1990s

Aardvarks

Although rarely used, the F-111 can accommodate an M61 Vulcan cannon in the bomb bay. This example has chalked up some 20 mm straffing time on the Red Flag Range. The colourful badge on the side of the fuselage confirms that this is an F-111 of the 27th TFW at Cannon AFB in New Mexico

PLASTIC TRANSPARENCIES
INSTALLED CONSULT
T.O. 1F-111A-2-2-1 FOR
SPECIAL CARE

ARMAMENTS
CARTS INST
CHAFF INST CHANNEL #3 10 EA

Above and right The F-111 is an impressive aircraft, with a span (wings fully spread) of 63 ft (19.2 m), and is some 73 ft 6 in (22.4 m) long. The E model is powered by a pair of P&W TF-30-3 turbofans each developing 19,600 lb (8891 kg) of thrust with afterburner. With the exception of the EF-111A electronic warfare variant, all F-111 models are in the Mach 2-plus class at altitude and can cruise automatically on the deck at 571 mph (919 km/h) during ingress to the target. Approaching the target area, however, the afterburners will be lit to push the Aardvark to near supersonic speed to achieve maximum surprise and (with luck) avoid being engaged by the defences

Left A Cannon-based F-111 carrying a Cubic Corporation ACMI pod for transmission of aerial data to computers on the ground. ACMI stands for Air Combat Manoeuvring Instrumentation; with this system an aerial engagement can be viewed in computer simulation on the ground or taped for later debrief by the pilots

The Aardvark tends to look ungainly from head-on. This view, together with the close-up on page 59, reveals the complex intake/wing geometry of the aircraft—especially the full-span slat along the leading edge and the glove vane and pivot junction configured for the minimum sweep position. The weapon pylons pivot as the wing sweeps back

These pages The 'Crusaders' of the 523rd TFS are one of the F-111 squadrons attached to the 27th TFW at Cannon

This page A Cannon-based F-111 turns onto final approach as the pilot backs off on the power and sets up for a landing. **Right** Burners glowing, an F-15 Eagle from Holloman AFB, New Mexico heads off to mix it with a strike package as an F-111F of the 48th TFW based at RAF Lakenheath in Great Britain makes the long journey to the runway. The F model is generally regarded as the best F-111 ever built

BUFFs

The B-52 isn't just a Big Ugly Fat
Fellow, it's a heavy smoker, too.
Red Flag exercises involve every
imaginable tactical asset in their
mock warfare scenarios. A B-52G
pollutes the atmosphere as it leaves
Nellis to fly an attack mission over
the imaginary Red Flag battle lines

Powered by its eight P&WA J57 turbojets, each generating 13,750 lb (6237 kg) of thrust, the B-52G on the preceding pages continues its climb out from Nellis. Note the bulges of the EVS (Electro-optical Viewing System) under the nose, a retrofit designed to improve target penetration in bad weather. **Right** Another B-52G departs from Nellis. The pilot's aren't wasting any time in retracting the gear: the outriggers are already up and the mains are just pivoting into the bays. Boeing built a total of 192 G models

Red Flag

Above Red Flag exercises are
organized four times a year by the
staff of the 4440th Tactical Fighter
Training Group in this building

Right Crew patch of the 57th
Fighter Weapons Wing, parent unit
of the Red Flag and Aggressor
squadrons

Main picture Each Red Flag
mission, with as many as 70 aircraft
over the range simultaneously, is
preceded by a mass briefing in the
Red Flag auditorium

The range control centre—code
name 'Blackjack'—has absolute
control over every Red Flag hop

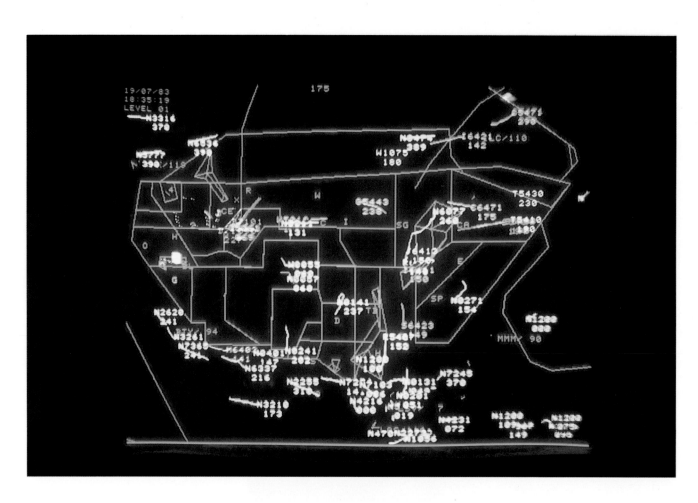

This computer map of the Red Flag
range displays the real-time location
and squawk number of each
participating aircraft in the exercise

The Aggressor pilots, flying on the 'red' or enemy side of the Red Flag war, are controlled by their own combat air controllers from one corner of the 'Blackjack' command centre

Ground threat radars, many of them mimicking the capabilities of Soviet anti-aircraft systems, bombard the Red Flag attackers with realistic emissions as they attempt to carry out their missions. **Right** An Air Force A-7K two-seater makes a 500-knot, 100-foot pass over a threat radar installation in the Nellis range

Preceding pages A pilot's eye view of the Nellis runways, with the flight line on the right. The Red Flag portion of the ramp is at the top of the picture. **These pages** A C-9 Nightingale hospital jet follows a Fighter Weapons School F-16 out for takeoff. Las Vegas is in the distance

A tiny portion of what is thought to be the world's largest patch collection in the parachute riggers' shop at Nellis. Hundreds of ultra-rare World War 2 patches are on display. Donations gladly accepted!

USAF Fighter Weapons School

Top left Headquarters of the Fighter Weapons School at Nellis. **Below and top right** The 64th and 65th Aggressor Squadrons work closely with the Fighter Weapons School as they simulate Soviet fighter tactics in their Northrop F-5E Tiger IIs. The F-5E is a small and simple fighter which has a performance envelope similar to the Mikoyan MiG-21 *Fishbed*. The Aggressors sport Soviet-style piped nose numbers and a wide variety of Eastern European and Third World camouflage schemes. **Bottom right** Detail of the Air Combat Manoeuvring Instrumentation system as it portrays a 2 v 2 dogfight

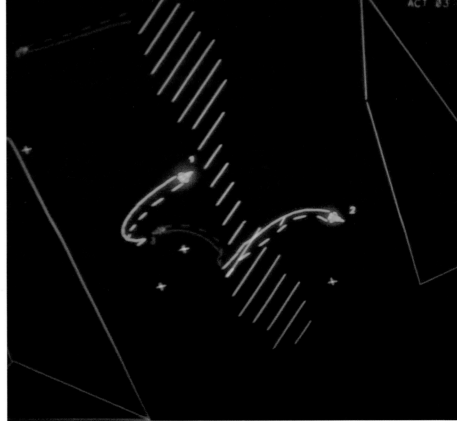

Preceding pages Multi-coloured
Aggressors lined up on the ramp;
the lofty control tower is visible on
the right of the main picture

These pages The F-5E has a punch in the nose (left) in the form of two 20 mm M-39A2 cannons with 280 rounds apiece. For training, a captive Sidewinder round is usually carried on the left wingtip for acquisition purposes. Aggressor F-5s also fly with ACMI data transmission pods (below left, in foreground). The wide track of the Tiger II's main gear is seen to advantage in this picture. The Aggressor squadrons are highly desired flying slots, and only the hottest Air Force fighter talent need apply. An Aggressor pilot gets set for an ACM mission (inset)

Preceding pages Aggressors take off to rendezvous over the range

These pages A rare opportunity to compare the contrasting colour schemes of the Aggressors in flight. This four-ship formation would be too unwieldy in a combat situation, so before the fight begins the formation will split into pairs for maximum flexibility and to minimize the risk of being spotted by a wary opponent

Eager Eagles

Main picture The twin tails of a
key Red Flag player, an F-15 Eagle
of the 33rd TFW out of Eglin AFB,
Florida. **Below** Nose well up, a 33rd
TFW Eagle bleeds off speed on final

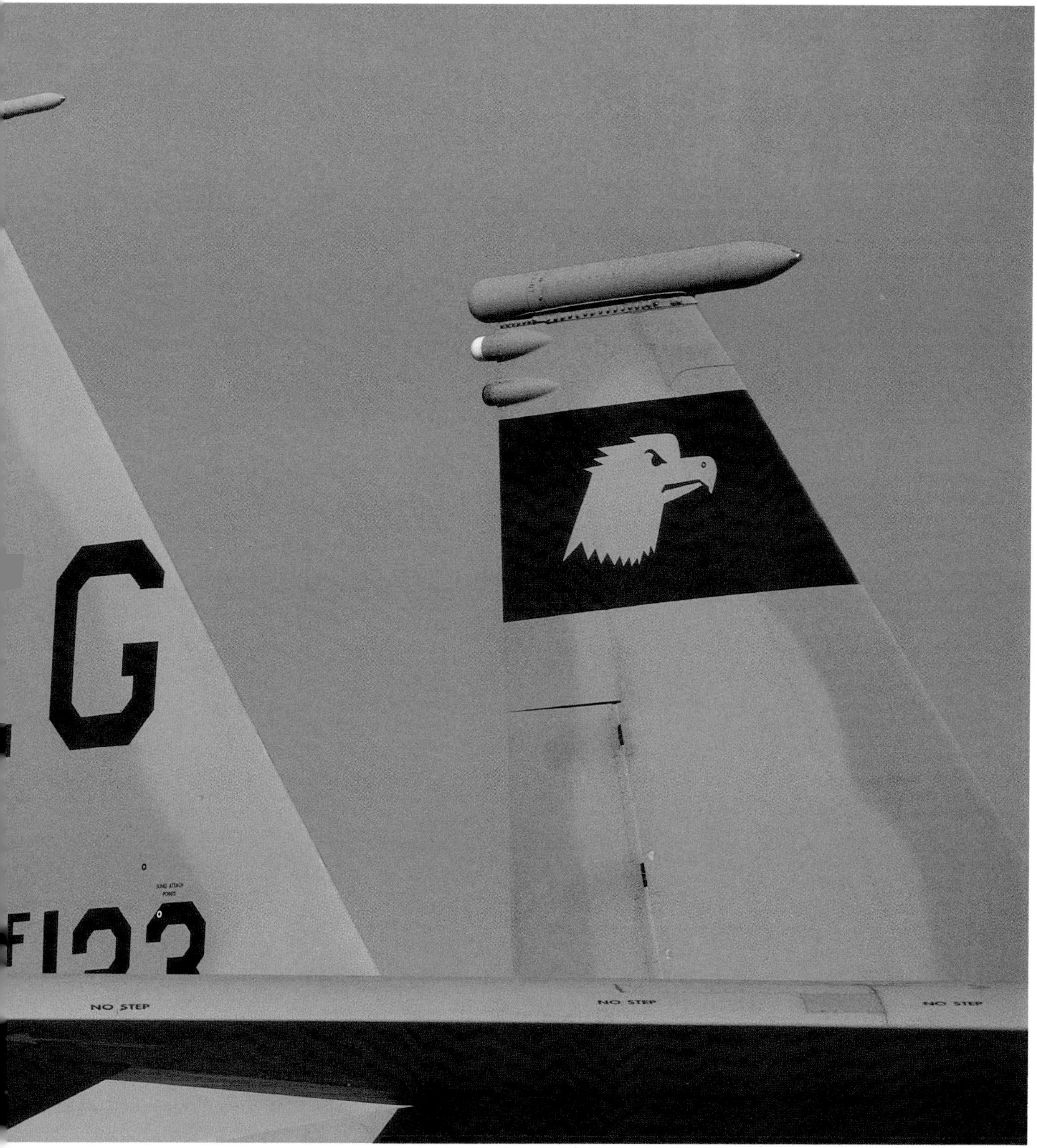

G
F123
NO STEP
NO STEP
NO STEP

The 33rd TFW is equipped with the F-15C, the first example of which first flew on 26 February 1979. Compared to the A model the F-15C has a greatly expanded radar detection/tracking capability, detail structural improvements to reduce complexity and weight, a large increase in both internal and external fuel capacities and considerably more multi-mission operability. Despite the new kid in fightertown in the shape of the F-16, the Eagle is still regarded by many as the ultimate assignment for any self-respecting fighter pilot

These pages Canopy polishing is no mere ritual, but an important part of preflight preparation: there are no marks for mistaking a bug for the bad guy

An Eagle driver gets under his
Stetson to protect his noggin from
the three-digit heat common at
Nellis

A returning Eagle displays the
standard air combat training
configuration of a Cubic data
transmission pod and a Sidewinder
acquisition round

Below The AIM-9L Sidewinder is the Eagle's standard short-range air-to-air missile, an infrared heat-seeker with an optimum range of about 3 miles (4.8 km)

Right Close-up of a captive Sidewinder missile and a Cubic data transmitter (nearest camera) fitted to an F-15. The aircraft has four fuselage stations for the semi-conformal carriage of the medium-range radar guided Sparrow air-to-air missile; one of the stations can be seen under the intake

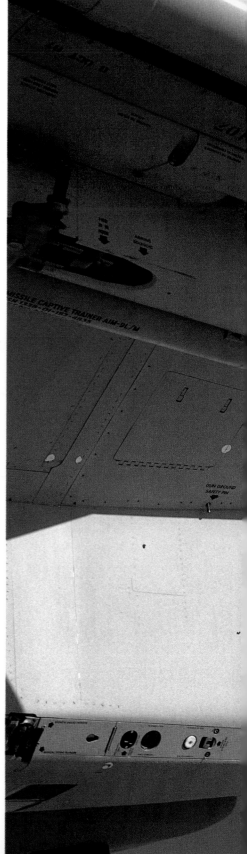

A perfect Eagle four-ship streaks into the landing
break over the Nellis runway

Birds of prey: the nearest Eagle is painted in a
prototype 'Europe One' camouflage scheme; similar
colouration will soon be seen on the first production
F-15E Strike Eagles

Fighting Falcons

These F-16s are well protected. Heavily-armed guards patrol the flight line; wander around without the proper authorization and escort, and you'll soon be licking the concrete. The red line symbolizes the fence that encloses flight lines at front-line tactical bases. All personnel and visitors must treat the red line as if it is a real fence— access to the flight line is allowed only at checkpoints about 100 metres apart. Anyone stepping over that little red rope will be arrested. No kidding

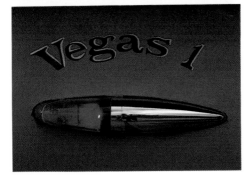

Main picture and **inset** Nellis hosts an entire F-16 wing in the 474th TFW. The unit badges of the wing's three squadrons adorn the commanding officer's F-16C

Above Detail of *City of North Las Vegas* and *Vegas 1*, both F-16s with the 474th TFW

An F-16 makes a full afterburner getaway from Nellis (left of picture) as the lights and casinos of Las Vegas twinkle and tinkle in the gathering darkness

An F-16 from Homestead AFB, Florida holds off as it prepares to land after a Red Flag hop. The aircraft is carrying combat tanks, Sidewinders and an ALQ-119 jammer

These F-16s came from Kunsan in
South Korea to compete in
Gunsmoke 1987. They belong to the
8th TFW

Some F-16 units have chosen to
decorate their mounts with a
stylized 'Fighting Falcon' motif

Main picture *Viper 5* of the 8th TFW sported a neat line in travel pods—his luggage obviously travels first class. **Far Left** Detail of the vertical stabilator of 81-714, 8th TFW

Line up of F-16 Fighting Falcons of the 419th TFW, Air Force Reserve, based at Hill AFB, Utah

HL
388TH TFW
AF 82 950

HL
388TH T
AF 82 006

Falcon tail feathers: 388th TFW, Hill AFB (main picture); 31st TFW, Homestead (inset); and 169th TFG, McEntire ANGB, South Carolina Air National Guard (above)

	ANG A-7 BUCKLEY ANGB, CO			
40 TFW				
TEAM TOTAL **8771**				
	BOX PAT'N	TAC PAT'N	NAV ATT'K	TOTAL
	728	675	650	2053
	723	719	852	2294
	621	690	884	2195
	719	642	868	2229
AD	2445	MAINT	6363	

	PACAF A-10 SUWON AB, KOREA			
51 TFW				
TEAM TOTAL **8514**				
	BOX PAT'N	TAC PAT'N	NAV ATT'K	TOTAL
PHILLIPS	748	431	817	1996
STEPHENSON	736	570	828	2134
DONISI	695	589	880	2164
HOY	722	678	820	2220
SANDERS				
WPNS LOAD	2860	MAINT	6397	

	USAFE A-10 RAF BENTWATERS, UK			
81 TFW				
TEAM TOTAL **8613**				
	BOX PAT'N	TAC PAT'N	NAV ATT'K	TOTAL
SPADA	705	586	848	2139
WICKSTROM	751	555	786	2092
SHRADER	696	676	832	2204
WIEBENER	797	501	880	2178
SCHWAB				
WPNS LOAD	2794	MAINT	6421	

GU

1

SKIFF

HUNTER

WAITTE

THOMAS

SENSENE

WPNS LO

NSMOKE 87

ANG	A-10	
BRADLEY ANGB, CT		

TFG

L 8298

TAC PAT'N	NAV ATTK	TOTAL
562	832	2112
483	847	2080
513	882	2079
596	710	2027

MAINT 6418

LEADER BOARD
AS OF 15 OCT

OVERALL

TOP TEAM	TOP GUN
388 TFW	HAMILTON 419 TFW

CATEGORY

TOP TEAM		TOP GUN
37 TFW	F-4	BREWER/LAVELLE 37 TFW
121 TFW	A-7	MCDAVID 140 TFW
81 TFW	A-10	HOY 51 TFW
388 TFW	F-16	HAMILTON 419 TFW

WPNS LOAD	MAINT
51 TFW	926 TFG

AAC	A-10
EIELSON AFB, AK	

343 TFW

TEAM TOTAL 7818

	BOX PAT'N	TAC PAT'N	NAV ATTK	TOTAL
MCHENRY	676	459	860	1995
JACKSON	686	466	788	1940
EMERSON	732	449	664	1845
BALL	689	571	778	2038
GIULIANO				

WPNS LOAD 23_ _INT 6421

TAC	
MYRTLE BEACH AFB	

354 TFW

TEAM TOTAL 8260

	BOX PAT'N	TAC PAT'N	NAV ATTK	T
ARMSTRONG	664	636	685	19
HICKS	641	615	710	19
BARTLEY	750	689	691	2
FLOUER	749	610	820	2
SMITH				

WPNS LOAD 2763   MAINT 638

Preceding spread The daily point totals are watched closely by all teams during the ten days of Gunsmoke

This page Maintenance crewmen attached to the 419th TFW, Air Force Reserve, previous repeat winners of Gunsmoke. The reservists had to settle for second place in 1987

The pitot head of a 31st TFW F-16
gets a final polish before a
Gunsmoke inspection

From front to back: the same
polisher shines the con/di nozzle of
the P&W F100-200 turbofan

Custom intake covers are hand-
made especially for the Gunsmoke
competition. This tasteful effort is
from the reservists of the 419th TFW
at Hill AFB

Air Force Reserve F-16s out of Hill
AFB, Ogden, Utah shine prior to
inspection by the Gunsmoke judges

F-16 crew chief salutes his pilot as
the jet heads out to the Gunsmoke
range

A C-9 Nightingale hospital ship of the Military airlift Command makes an evening landing at Nellis